Praise for *21 Ways to Add*

"*21 Ways to Add $100k to your Bus...*
Linette Montae has taken 21 business generating ideas...
feasible for the average entrepreneur to execute. The challenge is trying not to implement every idea at once. Dr. Montae communicates it so simply that you want to execute all 21. This is an easy read with actionable information and resources. There's a business building idea in this book for everyone."

Christy Demetrakis, The Empowered Speaker
EmpoweredSpeaker.com

As a seasoned business and marketing strategist who works with coaches, consultants, and entrepreneurs, I know so many people are trying to reach that elusive 6-figure mark. Linette's 21 Ways book makes it much easier to accomplish! I love that she included one of my favorite revenue-generating ideas: sponsorships. (I make much more than $100,000 with that one technique alone!) What's great is anyone who is looking to boost their income can find at least one tactic—probably many more— they can implement pretty quickly to start generating more revenue. Awesome book for any business owner.

Shannon Cherry, APR, MA founder of ShannonCherry.com, author of three
Amazon Bestsellers and creator of the SponsorshipMadeSimple.com program

"As a professional speaker and speech coach to experts, celebrities, and CEOs, I was familiar with many of these 21 Ways from doing them myself. What impressed me the most about this book is having all the creative Ways listed in one place, so you can easily and quickly create a strategy for exactly how anyone can plan to add an extra $100K to their business. Of course my favorite way is Way 9, but you'll find Ways for the beginner to the advanced business owner. The simple examples at the end of each Way bring the goal within reach and by combining several of these Ways, you can have fun while serving others and making money. Highly recommended!"

Felicia J. Slattery, M.A., M.Ad.Ed., author of *21 Ways to Make
Money Speaking* and creator of the Signature Speech™

"Wow, there is so much information and great advice that if you don't pick this up and start reading it now... you are missing out!"

Tonya Hofmann, CEO
PublicSpeakersAssociation.com

"As a business strategist, I help my clients create a plan for 'how' they're going to make $100,000, so I love *21 Ways to add $100K to Your Business*. Not only does Linette explain each money making idea, she also gives specific *$100K in One Year* examples for each Way. This book is great for new and seasoned entrepreneurs from all kinds of industries, especially those wanting to break the hours-for-dollars cycle. I will definitely recommend this book to my community.

Michele Scism, The 6 Figure Results Lady
DecisiveMinds.com

"If you've ever asked yourself, 'What else can I do to generate money for my solo business?' you've got to read *21 Ways to Add 100k To Your Business* by Dr. Linette Montae. No matter what type of solo professional you are, a newbie or seasoned entrepreneur, you will finish this book with a myriad of money-making strategies and ideas you can incorporate into your business model and sales funnel design—starting today! Get ready to expand your mind and think outside the box about what's possible to grow a six figure business."

Zenobia Garrison, M.A., C.C, Business Success Coach for Women/Launch While
You Work Strategist Success Transitions
SuccessTransitions.com

"Dr. Linette Montae is like a breath of fresh air in this 'How To ...' advice laden, online world. When she enters your life, get ready for your confusion to clear; for your overwhelm to melt away; and for your business to seriously take off. With her lightning quick mind and a bucketful of inspirational wisdom, Dr. Linette can pinpoint your pain point in an instant and transform it into brilliantly clear, tailor made business systems and processes that get awesome results for your workload, your sanity and your wallet!"

Isabel Gainford, Branding Coach Extraordinaire
IsabelGainford.com

"Before I started coaching with Linette, I knew I wanted to start a business outside of my medical practice but I couldn't figure out how to turn my ideas into money. After working with Linette, I have a solid plan for products and programs, and I am preparing to host my first live event. Speaking is something I always wanted to do so I am really excited."

Dr. Adekemi Oguntala (Dr. O), The Clinicians Coach
TheTeenDoc.com

21 Ways to Add $100,000 to Your Business

21 WAYS

to **add**

$100,000

to your **business**

Dr. Linette Montae

Discover! BOOKS™
an Imprint of Imagine! Books™

High Point, North Carolina

21 Ways™ Series, Book 9

Published by Discover! Books™
an Imprint of Imagine! Books™
PO Box 16268, High Point, NC 27261
contact@artsimagine.com

Imagine! Books™ is an enterprise of Imagine! Studios™
Visit us online at www.artsimagine.com

ISBN 13: 978-1-937944-14-8

First Discover! Books™ printing, April 2013

Dedication

To all the small business entrepreneurs who are stuck in the hours-for-dollars business model.

Introduction

For most passionate entrepreneurs, money isn't the most important thing. *But* you need to accept that money touches everything that is important. Like the title of my first book says, *Passion Won't Pay The Bills*.

There are really only three primary steps to increase your business income

✓ Get more customers

✓ Repeatedly sell to your existing customers

✓ Raise your rates

This can be done by creating *new* products and programs, and by adding services, while other times you can simply repurpose what you have and offer it in a different way.

Remember:

✓ People learn in different ways

✓ People want options that fit their lifestyle

✓ People want options that fit their budget

Each Way in this book will give you an example of how you can make $100,000 with that Way in one year. This is designed to get you started. The magic happens when you mix and match various Ways to make $100,000.

It's not as hard as you may think.

It's just a formula.

Committed to your success,

Dr. Linette Montae

WAY 1

Teleseminars

Teleseminars are one of my absolute favorite ways to create a new program or product. First, let me explain what a teleseminar is. You may have heard the words teleseminar, teleconference, tele-call, tele-training. There are a lot of terms used to describe this particular opportunity, but no matter what the word they all simply mean you are going to use the telephone to share information.

The information you share is usually some type of learning, growing, or developmental experience for the person listening. A teleseminar can be done live or as a recording.

The first thing you need is a telephone bridge line. I'm sure you have been on a conference call at least once in your life, perhaps at your job where people located in different places attended a staff or board meeting via telephone. A teleseminar works with the same principle as a conference call. All you need is a conference line so people can call in and talk to you, listen to you, or both. The awesome thing about conferencing lines is they are available for free. While there are conference bridge lines that cost, there is no need to pay for one to host a teleseminar. The average free conference bridge service will give you about 200 lines, which is usually enough if you're just getting started. As your business grows you may need more than 200 lines and in that case you can certainly upgrade to the paid version to gain additional space, but for now let's not worry about that. Check out FreeConferenceCall.com, FreeConferenceCalling. com, and FreeConferencePro.com for some options. Once you have signed up for your free conference bridge line, you're ready to go. The conference bridge service will provide you with a telephone number and a pass code that is unique to you so people can call in and listen to your training.

The best teleseminars are about 60 minutes long. You simply choose a popular topic within your industry, invite people to attend your teleseminar, share your awesome content, and record the training. The conference bridge line will automatically create an MP3 you can download to your computer and instantly put up for sale. You can sell the MP3 download of your workshop directly to virtual customers and you can also turn the MP3 download into a physical CD that can be purchased and mailed to your customer.

Sounds easy, right? It's just as easy as I explained it, so choose a topic and get started!

Take Action:

✓ Create one teleseminar and host it to a live audience.

✓ Host a teleseminar series featuring other experts in your niche.

✓ Have the MP3 audio file transcribed and offer a package that includes the audio and the transcription. *Keep in mind that some people like to listen, some like to read, and some like both.*

✓ Increase the value by creating an action guide to go along with the MP3 or the CD audio.

How to Make $100K in One Year Example:

Sell 3,703 audio and transcript packages of your teleseminar on your website for $27 each.

Resources in this Way:

 FreeConferenceCall

 FreeConferenceCalling

 FreeConferencePro

WAY 2

Video Courses

Thanks to YouTube, video has grown in popularity and it's very easy to do. No longer will you need a professional videographer, professional equipment and loads and loads of money to create an awesome video. With the quality of smart phone cameras, you can record a professional looking video with your cell phone. There are also inexpensive video cameras available (Kodak offers a great model) and you can even use your computer's webcam.

Keeping in mind that people learn in different ways, video accomplishes three major goals:

✓ It allows you to build a relationship with current and prospective customers a lot faster than words on paper or a computer screen.

✓ It is great for people who like to learn by watching.

✓ Once you have a video, you can always strip the audio and repurpose the information as an MP3 or CD.

Right now you may be thinking, "I absolutely do not want to be on camera," and I respect that more than you know. I, too, had a fear of being on camera. Let me assure you, being on camera is not that bad and you do get used to the experience, but there are other ways to do video without you having to be seen.

Live Video

You can create a video with you speaking live to the viewer. Although this can be scary, it is probably the best way to quickly build a relationship, and remember the relationship is what causes your prospective and current clients to pull out their wallets and buy. With this method you can create short, two- to three-minute long videos, fifteen- to twenty-minute long instructional videos, or in-depth training videos that are sixty to ninety minutes long. People tend to have a short attention span and very little time, so when choosing longer videos it is critical to consider your topic, your audience, and your purpose for that video.

Screen Cast Video

You can create a PowerPoint presentation (PowerPoint.com), record the audio for your PowerPoint and turn it into a video. This is very easy to do if you have PowerPoint 2010 or later, as previous versions are not as easy to turn into a video. I use the PowerPoint-to-video technique fairly often because it gives me three things at once: a PowerPoint presentation, an audio I can use as a product, and the video for tips or a larger product. I bet you have some PowerPoint presentations already in your computer that you can simply record the audio and turn into a video right away. When using this method, it's a good idea to pay attention to slide transitions. I also encourage you to use more images than words to keep the video interesting and visually appealing for your viewer. The length of the video when using this method still needs to be considered for the same reasons as the live video method.

The Slideshow Video

Third, you can create a video using animation. This opportunity is a little bit harder to explain and is probably best understood after seeing one in action. An animation video is a video using pictures and text to share your message (check out Animoto.com). It's not generally used for sharing content, but more appropriate when you want to impart a single concept. Animated videos are usually between thirty seconds and two minutes long. I have seen some animation videos that were longer, but that is an advanced strategy.

Take Action:

✓ Create one video and embed it on your website.

✓ Create a video series and upload each video to YouTube.

✓ Create an action guide to go with your video or video series and sell it as a product.

✓ Offer the video as a download or physical DVD.

How to Make $100K in One Year Example:

Sell 508 video and action guide products on your website for $197 each.

Resources in this Way:

Microsoft PowerPoint

Animoto

WAY 3

Workshops & Breakout Sessions

Even in this virtual world, people still love face-to-face workshops. This is a great way to increase your visibility. You can offer workshops for businesses, educational institutions, community groups, and conferences. There are plenty of opportunities for you to offer a workshop or breakout session.

So what can you share?

You know a lot of things that other people don't know. If you don't already have a list of topics you could easily teach in a workshop format, I recommend you take out a piece of paper and brainstorm a list of all the things you know and could teach others. Be careful not to discount topics you think everyone already knows because there's always a group of people who don't know something you do. What you know may come easy to you, but often what comes easiest to you is a major struggle for others. An easy way to do this exercise is to keep track of questions people ask that you're always answering.

Now that you have your list, choose three to five topics you would enjoy presenting. To best support your business growth it's a good idea to select topics that flow well together or topics that can build upon each other. Once you have your core topics, all that's left to do is create the content. Workshops and breakout sessions can vary in length, but generally span from 45 to 90 minutes. If you are presenting for someone else, they will let you know how much time you have. If you are offering the workshop alone, consider creating workshops that are between 60 and 120 minutes long.

Take Action:

✓ The longer the workshop, the more interactive it should be. Include activity times for your audience to take action on what they have learned.

✓ Use the Internet to search for conferences, because they often need breakout speakers. The best way to search for a conference is to type in your topic and add the word, "conference." For example, "women entrepreneur conference." Search for conferences regularly so you don't miss important call for presenter submission deadlines.

✓ Offer one workshop or a series of workshops that build upon each other.

How to Make $100K in One Year Example:

Sell 337 seats at a series of live workshops for $297 each. Offer a day long intensive workshop at 200 conferences and charge $500 for each one.

WAY 4

Homestudy Courses

Think of a home study course as learning in a box. A home study course can be delivered virtually as a downloadable product or as a physical product delivered to the customer. A home study course can be written material, audio, video, or any combination. You can create a home study course from scratch or use existing content collecting dust on your hard drive.

The fastest and easiest way to create a home study course is to repurpose something you already have. That means taking a teleseminar, MP3, CD, or video you have already done (see Ways 1 and 2) and packaging the material in a different way so the learner can work through your information at their own pace. For example, you previously offered a live six-part teleseminar series. You originally made money by offering the teleseminar series live and now you can use the recordings of the teleseminar series as a home study course or package it with transcripts, an action guide, or videos. Check out Odesk.com and Elance.com for outsourcing tasks like transcription, action guide creation, video editing and audio cleanup.

The main focus of home study courses is to give customers the ability to learn from you when *they* have time. A home study course also gives them the opportunity to listen, read, or view over and over again, which is not an option when you do a live class. Sometimes people who attended your live class will want your information for years to come and will purchase the home study version, and sometimes buyers are people who could not attend the live teaching. In either case, you have created an opportunity for another income stream by providing your information in a home study format.

How to Make $100K in One Year Example:

Charge $97 to 500 people for your live series and then sell 104 copies of your home study course for $497 each.

Resources in this Way:

 Odesk

 Elance

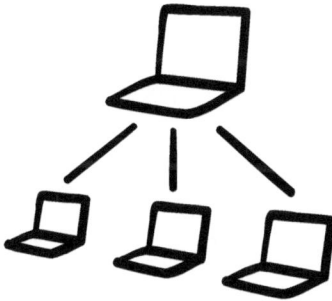

WAY 5

Group Coaching

One of the challenges with providing one-on-one coaching is that it puts a ceiling on your business income. Coaching is generally an hour-for-dollars business, which means you coach, you get paid, you coach, you get paid, you coach, you get paid. Now that may sound like a great idea and it will bring money into your business, however you only have 24 hours in a day, so once your coaching slots are filled you have no time for new clients, which translates to no more money.

The problem with coaching in its purest form is the business model you use. Group coaching is an option that helps you serve more clients and make more money because you are not devoting your time to one person at a time.

Because group coaching is done with more than one person at a time, the price point for group coaching is lower than traditional one-on-one coaching. This allows more people to access your knowledge while keeping within smaller budgets. Group coaching members also benefit because they are supported by the ideas of everyone in the group. Yes, you are the coach, but be careful not to think so highly of yourself as to believe your members can only grow from your wisdom. Participants of group coaching programs have consistently reported increased value from being in a group of like-minded people working together to accomplish similar goals and supporting one another's efforts.

Group coaching can be done in person or virtually. It can be done by e-mail, audio, video, telephone, and online forums. A group coaching program can last one month, three months, six to nine months, or even twelve months. The length of the program should be based on the content you deliver, the skills your clients need to develop, or the number of actions the group members need to perform to be successful. For example, I taught a live six-week tele-seminar series. During this series I gave the attendees all the information they needed to take action, however some people need more than information. They need hand-holding and accountability, or they may just like to ask questions and bounce ideas around while they take action. So I created a group coaching program to support those who wanted more of my help than the six-week tele-seminar provided. After looking at the information shared in the six-week tele-seminar series and all of the steps involved in implementing each of the six pillars taught, I determined it would take one month to implement each pillar, making the group coaching program six months long. The goal of this group coaching program was to actually get it done, not to teach them new information. Although content delivery could be appropriate for group coaching, it was not the goal for this particular program.

There are so many ways to structure a group coaching program I couldn't possibly cover them all in detail, so I will share how I structured the six-month group coaching program I've been discussing. First, I assumed members of the group had already attended the live six-week teleseminar series or purchased the home study version so the group coaching program did not begin with entry-level discussion. However, it was possible for a brand-new person to follow along using the home study version as a guide throughout the six-month group coaching program. I like to keep things as simple as possible for everyone, so I structured the program to offer a 60 to 90 minute live teleseminar at the beginning of each month where I detailed what they would focus on that month. They also received a comprehensive action guide for implementation based on their level of knowledge, skills, and business development. To provide individual attention to each member's questions and concerns, I chose to offer open office hours via telephone and daily e-mail access to me. However, there are a number of ways you can support group coaching members' unique challenges.

That was just one example of a group coaching program and the design can be even easier. In its purest form, group coaching can be a six-month program where you meet twice a month. Of course I prefer you meet virtually, but in-person meetings work just as well for some markets. In one meeting you can deliver high quality content and the second meeting can be a live Q&A where the group members get to ask questions and share tips, tools, and resources with one another. You can record both monthly sessions and provide the MP3 to your members in case they were not able to attend live or would just like the opportunity to listen again. You always have the option of adding value by creating transcripts or action guides, but they are not necessary and should be determined based on the price point you set for your group coaching program.

How to Make $100K in One Year Example:

Run a six-week group coaching program five times in one year. Charge $1,997 per person to attend and cap the number of attendees at ten people. Fifty people times $1,997 equals almost $100,000 in one year.

WAY 6

Membership Programs

I bet at some point in your life you have been a member of a group, organization, or club. People really like being part of a bigger cause, as it makes them feel connected. It doesn't have to be a large association to be a membership program. You can create a VIP club or an Inner Circle or whatever you want to call it. You can create a membership program that is face-to-face or virtual. Keep in mind it takes less time to set up a virtual program that practically runs on automatic pilot than it does to travel to a location and teach.

The two most common forms of membership programs are perpetual or fixed term. They each have pros and cons to consider. A perpetual membership program is one that continues month after month or year after year until the member cancels. A fixed term membership has a specific end date. The challenge with membership programs is keeping the members interested, engaged, and paying. Statistically, members begin to lose interest or stop seeing the value of a membership program somewhere around month three or four. If you have an on-going membership program it increases the likelihood that members will leave. But if you choose a fixed term membership, let's say a six-month program, a member who may begin losing interest around month three or four will likely stick it out because they know the end is in sight. As a result, as both a seller and a purchaser, I prefer fixed term membership programs.

There are also two common forms of membership program payments and each has its advantages and disadvantages. The traditional membership program is an annual investment. Those are things like associations in which you usually pay once a year for twelve months' worth of benefits. Then there's what I like to call the meeting model, where members pay by-the-month. Here again you need to be crystal clear on your reason for the membership program, how you're going to use the program, the target market for the program, the program price point, and whether it will be perpetual or fixed term.

The disadvantage of once-a-year membership dues is only getting money once a year *and* it will be twelve months before you know if the member is going to renew. You could have a member who has been unhappy with the program since month five, but because they already paid for the whole year they stay and you never know their intention to leave until it's possibly too late to salvage the relationship. What I love about the meeting model is the consistent, more predictable monthly income it provides. Not to mention it helps program prospects who are financially challenged.

You may be familiar with membership programs that meet face-to-face weekly or monthly like girl scouts, rotary club, or book clubs. That same concept can be applied to a virtual membership and is often delivered via a password secured website or private forum.

How to Make $100K in One Year Example:

Create a low-end fixed term membership site for $10 per month for three months. Sell 3,334 memberships. Create a high-end fixed term membership site for $97 per month for three months. Sell 344 memberships. Create an ongoing membership site for $10 per month and offer a 5% discount for annual payments. Sell either 833 ongoing memberships, 877 annual memberships, or a combination of both.

WAY **7**

Author

When you hear the word author, you may immediately think of a physical book, but there are many ways to make money as an author. Here are five opportunities to write and make money:

Physical Book

Writing a book is probably the first thing you think of when you hear the word, "author," and it may also be the furthest thing from your to-do-list, but it is certainly worth considering. There are two things I want to share regarding publishing a physical book that I hope helps you see this option in a more positive light. First, a physical book no longer needs to be 500 pages that takes you ten years to write and get published.

Nowadays the goal of a book is to showcase your expertise and increase your visibility. In order to showcase your expertise, it needs to be a book your prospective clients will actually pick up, read, and finish. It doesn't help you or them if the book is so long they never get to that end. Honestly, books between 100 and 200 pages in length are extremely popular. Second, it has also become commonplace for an author to self-publish their book. No longer is it seen as taboo or less respectable, *if* it is done with high quality.

With these two pieces of information in hand, the thought of writing a physical book should no longer cause you to shake in your boots. As a matter of fact, I always push my clients to write a book. Understand up front that book sales alone will not immediately make you $100,000. There are very few people in the world who have enough book sales to directly bring in that kind of money, but there are other kinds of business a published book will bring that makes this opportunity extremely attractive. There is something magical about being able to say you are an author. People look at you differently, they trust you differently, they respect you differently—it's just different.

E-book

A physical book is great, but I respect that it is not for everyone so another way to package your expertise is by writing an e-book. Now I have to tell you the truth, by the time you write a thirty- to fifty-page e-book, you probably could have just kept writing and produced enough information for that physical book you're dodging.

So what exactly is an e-book? "E-book" stands for "electronic" book, so the basis of an e-book is the fact that it is not a physical book you go into a bookstore or a library to obtain. Rather an e-book is delivered in a downloadable format. The terminology and popularity of e-books has changed with the invention of e-book readers like the Kindle and iPad, which is how many people now enjoy consuming information. The great thing about e-books is they are extremely inexpensive to produce and once your e-book is ready for sale, collecting the money and delivering the product happens on auto-pilot. Depending upon the level of technical information included in your e-book, it can sell for anywhere from several dollars to several hundred dollars. The other huge advantage of an e-book is that it satisfies your customers' immediate need. With a physical book your potential customer has to wait for the book to arrive or they have to go to the store to purchase the book. An e-book is downloaded instantly and they can begin reading it immediately.

For more information on book writing and publishing, check out Kristen Eckstein's book in this series, *21 Ways to Write & Publish Your Non-Fiction Book*.

Special Report

A special report is very much like an e-book in content. The biggest difference is the method of delivery and sometimes the length. A special report is generally information you create in a Word document, turn into a PDF and is available for immediate download from your website. A special report can be three to five pages or as long as thirty to fifty pages and the price can range from $7 to $97 depending upon the length, the content, and of course your reputation.

Ghostwriting

Another opportunity for you to make money as an author is to write for someone else. If you love to write and are an excellent writer, there are a lot of opportunities for you to write on behalf of someone else. You can write someone's physical book, e-book, or special report based on information they provide. You can also get paid to write blog posts and short articles. Ghostwriters, in fact, can make a nice chunk of change depending on the topic or end product. For example, a ghost writer for a physical book between 100 and 200 pages can make between $3,000 and $10,000. Keep in mind the rate you are able to charge as a ghostwriter is going to be based on your skill, speed, and ability to capture an author's voice and translate that into the written word. Ghostwriters who excel in these areas are well compensated and in high demand.

How to Make $100K in One Year Example:

Sell 5,000 copies of your book for $20 each. Sell 10,000 copies of your eBook for $10 each. Sell 1,031 special reports for $97 each. Ghostwrite ten books for $10,000 each.

Resources in this Way:

 *21 Ways to Write & Publish Your Non-Fiction Book* by Kristen Eckstein

WAY 8

Webinars

A webinar is another opportunity to deliver your information in a way that is convenient and appealing to your prospective clients. Think of a webinar as delivering a PowerPoint presentation virtually. A webinar has its greatest advantage in the fact that people can attend from anywhere in the world as long as they can connect to the Internet. A webinar also allows you to share visual information so attendees can watch and absorb more than they can just hearing your voice on a teleseminar.

A lot of webinar services offer additional tools that can enhance your presentation and increase the enjoyment of your attendees. For example, many webinar services offer a chat room. This allows your attendees to interact with you and one another throughout the presentation. This feature allows both you and them to ask questions. It's almost like being in a live face-to-face workshop without the face (See AdobeConnectPro.com and Hangout.Google.com).

Some of the really good webinar services like GoToWebinar (GoToWebinar.com) also offer the opportunity for attendees to share their screen with everyone else. Some services even allow attendees to appear live via webcam where everyone, including you, can watch. A service like that would also allow you to be seen live, if you want to be visible instead of or in addition to a slide style presentation. Some webinars have a whiteboard and highlighter which gives your presentation a classroom feeling. Many of the webinar services provide an audio and/or video record option which you can later download and turn into a product. You can offer the product as a virtual download, give access to it on your website, and/or burn it to a DVD and offer the physical product. Like teleseminars, you can do one webinar alone or a webinar series. You can also increase the value of your webinars by adding transcripts, an action guide, or even a Q&A session.

The one thing I would like to caution you about regarding webinars is the technical comfort level you have with using virtual tools of this nature. I recommend my private clients begin with a tele-seminar because almost everyone is comfortable using a telephone. A webinar has quite a few buttons and gadgets you may not be ready for right out the gate. I don't want you to be afraid, I just want you to be aware and not attempt to do a webinar next week when you've never done one before. I suggest you sign up for a free webinar service or free trial and spend time tinkering around. Figure out exactly how it all works and which buttons to press so when you deliver the webinar live, especially if you charge people to attend, you are not embarrassed or setting yourself up for a high refund request rate.

How to Make $100K in One Year Example:

Host a webinar and turn it into a home study course that offers transcripts, video, audio, an action guide, and a bonus Q&A session with you. Sell 200 copies for $497 each.

Resources in this Way:

GoToWebinar

Adobe Connect Pro

Google Hangout

WAY 9

Speaking

Much like the thought of being an author, public speaking is an idea that causes many people to shake in their boots. You may be one of those people. I certainly remember how I felt the first time I stood in front of a room full of people who were watching my every word and move. Even as a national speaker I still get nervous every single time I step on stage. If you're willing to push through your fear, you can make a lot of money as a speaker.

There are two main roads to speaking: speaking for free and for a fee. Let's start with the easiest one to explain. Speaking for a fee is pretty self-explanatory. You have a workshop or keynote that you deliver and you are paid to do so. The key is to find a message people both want to hear and are willing to pay for. Sounds simple, but it is not necessarily that easy. Here's where having a physical book can really help you get paid speaking gigs (see Way 7). The second option is speaking for free. I know that doesn't sound like a strong road to $100,000, but when done correctly it is very possible to make more money speaking for free than when you speak for a fee.

Standing in front of ten people or ten thousand people is not the difficult part of being a financially successful speaker. Opening your mouth and sharing information that will help others is only one component of being a speaker. The second component is being a good marketer. Your website, speaker one sheet, speaker brochure, and demo video need to be carefully crafted if you want speaking to be a healthy part of your business. I had a coach who often said, "As a speaker you need to look like you cost twice as much as you charge," which means you cannot have an amateur looking website and you cannot create speaking materials on your home computer.

The best way to get started in the speaking industry is to reach out to groups, organizations, clubs, and educational institutions in your community. Organizations like the Rotary Club schedule speakers to present at their monthly meetings. Whether you speak for free or for a fee, you should make an offer to the attendees. For example, you can focus on increasing your email list by inviting the attendees to get your free e-book. Or you can invite the attendees to register for your upcoming teleseminar which will go into greater detail on the topic you just shared with them.

Caution: My goal is to give you a simplistic glimpse into the world of making money whether you speak for a fee or for free. My explanation is extremely basic and does not cover all the steps involved in the process. For that I recommend Felicia Slattery of Communication Transformation at LinetteRecommends.com/felicia. You can also check out her book in this series, *21 Ways to Make Money Speaking*.

How to Make $100K in One Year Example:

Charge $4,200 each time you speak for a fee and land two speaking gigs each month.

Speak for free and sell a high ticket coaching or mastermind program from the stage (see Ways 5, 13 and 19).

Resources in this Way:

 Felicia Slattery, Communication Transformation

 *21 Ways to Make Money Speaking* by Felicia Slattery

Newsletters

You would be amazed how many people are willing to pay a monthly fee for subscription-based newsletters. Like with anything else, the amount you charge for a newsletter subscription is based on the amount and quality of information you provide. People in highly technical industries can offer newsletter subscriptions for hundreds of dollars. Medical and legal newsletters also command a high dollar. You may be in an industry that will subscribe to a paid newsletter, but perhaps your newsletter is $9.97 or $17 a month.

The other factor to consider when pricing your newsletter is the mode of delivery. A newsletter delivered virtually will likely have a lower price tag than a newsletter physically mailed to your subscriber. Likewise, the visual quality of the newsletter can also affect the subscription price. A folded black and white newsletter will not command as high an asking price as a full color newsletter on white semi-gloss paper that arrives in an envelope already three-ring hole punched. Lastly, the length of the newsletter is to be considered. A four-page newsletter will not command the same subscription rate as a twenty-page newsletter.

Virtual newsletters have become extremely popular for many reasons. First, the delivery via e-mail or download is convenient via a service like Aweber.com. Second, the subscriber can read virtual newsletters on a computer screen and print at their discretion. Third, a virtual newsletter is more cost-effective for you because it does not have printing and postage expense. Fourth, virtual newsletters can be saved on your subscriber's computer—no dust and no clutter. Fifth, you can save time and energy by outsourcing the tasks involved in the creation and delivery of your newsletter.

Unless you are a graphic designer, I encourage you to invest in an expert designer to create your newsletter template. You really want a professional looking product that matches your brand and showcases your value. Once the template has been created, write the content and insert. If you don't like to write you can hire a ghost writer to produce the content and you can pay someone to insert the content, add images or quotes, and make the finished product look and feel great. Hint: Be sure your newsletter template includes a call to action—an offer that gives your reader an opportunity to purchase something else.

How to Make $100K in One Year Example:

Create a monthly paper newsletter in a highly trained and targeted niche and sell 1,031 subscriptions for $97 per month.

Create a lower-end digital newsletter and sell 5,882 subscriptions for $17 per month.

Resources in this Way:

Aweber for virtual newsletters

Sponsors

Not many people realize this income stream is available or recognize it as appropriate for an entrepreneur. I know being a small business owner I never considered having sponsors until my eyes were opened to the possibilities. Sponsors are not just looking for famous people or big businesses to help promote their products and services. They need people just like you and me.

The bottom line goal of a sponsor is to get their products or services in the hands of their target market. For example, let's say you are a parenting coach. There are a whole bunch of products on the market targeted at parents: Everything from juice boxes and disposable diapers to cribs and happy meals. If a company is interested in reaching parents of toddlers and preschoolers and you can offer direct access to a ton of those parents, a sponsor will be interested in hearing your proposal.

Think about it this way: Commercials are extremely expensive and they are not guaranteed to reach the target market a product is designed to serve. That being the case, any savvy business would rather pay you $10,000 to share or allow them to share their product with your community than spend $100,000 on a sixty-second commercial that may or may not be seen by the kind of parents they want.

Consider this... When you pick up a magazine, have you noticed how at least half of the magazine is advertising? Have you also noticed how the ads in the magazine offer products the readers of that magazine would likely be interested in purchasing? A savvy business owner would not put an ad for Pampers® in an issue of *Newsweek*. That doesn't mean the readers of *Newsweek* never purchase Pampers®, it's just not the highest probability for the advertisers to see a return on investment.

When you look to get sponsors, you need to know what you have to offer and you also need to be crystal clear as to the market the potential sponsor wants to reach. Once you understand what the sponsor wants, your next step is to show how you can help them achieve their goal. And you can't do it with lip service; you need to give them data. For example, how many readers or subscribers do you have in your potential sponsor's target market subscribed to your newsletter? For entrepreneurs who have a huge readership, you may be in the position to offer a sponsor access to a market they really want to reach. What about on social media—do you have a huge Twitter or Facebook following that actively engages you and your content?

Now that I have your brain juices flowing, begin considering what types of products or services you and your typical clients use or would find beneficial. Once you have a list of those products and/or services, you can look for companies that offer those things and identify whether their target market is a match for the clients and customers you can give them access to. Also check out my friend Shannon Cherry's *Sponsorship Made Simple* course at LinetteRecommends.com/shannon

How to Make $100K in One Year Example:

Get ten sponsors at $10,000 each or two sponsors for $50,000 each.

Resources in this Way:

 Shannon Cherry's Sponsorship training program

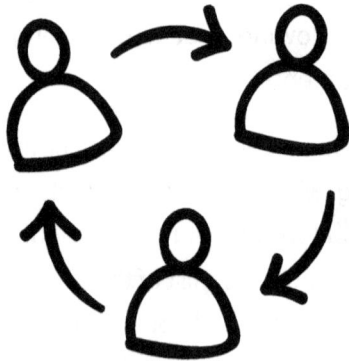

WAY 12

Subscriptions

We have already talked about membership programs and newsletters (see Ways 6 and 12), so what's left?

Let's talk about the continuity model—a membership type that deserves a dedicated Way. Like a traditional membership program, a continuity subscription can be perpetual or fixed term. However, the strength of the continuity model is its basis in monthly payments.

Depending on what you offer in your continuity program, the investment can range from $9.97 a month to $1997 a month and beyond. Since a continuity subscription program is about giving something every month, you have the opportunity to make adjustments along the way as you engage your members and learn what they need to remain happy with their investment. So if you know that statistically months three and four can be problematic for member retention, structure your continuity program to deliver a really awesome unannounced bonus in month three.

Note: The most popular frequency is monthly, but a continuity subscription can be weekly, bimonthly, or even quarterly.

To help you grasp the continuity concept, think about a monthly CD or DVD club. What about a book-of-the-month club? Those are subscription continuity programs in their purest form and a lot of people still enjoy them. Even with the popularity of the Internet, people still subscribe to magazines and "of the month" clubs.

So what can you offer in a continuity program? Sure, you can sell monthly downloads, teleseminars, or even a monthly Q&A call, but studies have shown continuity programs with a physical product to be the most successful. That can be a CD, DVD, or another resource sent by postal mail. Consider your prospects' problems and brainstorm how you can solve them. Don't discount any ideas you come up with. Who ever thought Beanie Babies® could be sold in a continuity program? By golly, it's a stuffed animal! The person with that idea made a boatload of money.

The key to a profitable continuity program is not the price tag for the monthly subscription; it's the number of subscribers. A continuity program is a lot like compound interest. Receiving $37 per month from one person is nothing to run to the bank over, but when you have 226 subscribers for 12 months, you have made $100K. Is *that* worth a trip to the bank? I don't know your target market, but I am willing to bet that out of a billion people, you can find 226 who will happily subscribe to your monthly continuity program. As previously mentioned, your subscription amount will be based on the product, delivery, and technical level of the content. Sure, the higher the subscription, the more money you can make, but don't make a mistake following greed. Your prospects will not buy if your offer is overpriced and they will not stay if you fail to provide value. I recommend you over deliver and surprise your subscribers to entice them to remain paying customers.

How to Make $100K in One Year Example:

Sell a $9.97 per month membership to 836 subscribers. Sell a $37 per month subscription to 226 subscribers.

WAY 13

Mastermind Programs

A mastermind is a small group of people who support one another with ideas, tips, tools, and resources for success. The best thing about belonging to a mastermind group is benefiting from the wisdom of several people. I even have coaching clients who prefer my mastermind program over doing private sessions with me.

Don't be insulted if you encounter a similar situation. Your goal is to help your client achieve success. That does not mean every answer has to come from you. Actually when you get over your ego, it is very freeing to not feel like you must have a solution to your client's every problem.

A mastermind group can meet in person, by telephone, online, or by video. The most common meeting method seems to be telephone. The most effective masterminds have four to eight people in a group. You can have as many groups as you need, but keeping each mastermind small allows individuals plenty of time to share and get help.

Most masterminds have a structure that everyone agrees to follow. For example, if you offer a four-person mastermind group that meets for one hour every week, each person basically gets fifteen minutes. Believe it or not, that is enough time if everyone comes prepared and remains focused. This is not the time for chit chat—it is a time to bring a problem before the group and get suggestions that can help solve the issue at hand. It also helps if each person brings only one problem to the table at a time.

As the leader, you can facilitate the mastermind group or you can let them function on their own. The last mastermind group I offered was a mixture of the two options. The group met for three weeks alone and on the fourth week I facilitated the group. You can also offer high-end masterminds where you are always present, but as you can imagine, the member investment should be steep.

There are many ways to put a twist on the mastermind concept, but keep in mind that your time is valuable. When you begin doing masterminds, it's easy for you to be there for every meeting, but as your business grows it will become increasingly impossible. One of my coaches said, "Make decisions today as if you were already making $1,000,000." If you think this way in your business, you can plan programs that leave room for growth. Caution: Very few people have been successful at leading large in-person masterminds. It can be done, but really takes skill and precision because you want everyone to get the help and guidance they need from the experience they paid to receive. If you're new to facilitating masterminds, start virtual and expand from there.

How to Make $100K in One Year Example:

Offer a ninety-day virtual mastermind to ten people every three months for $2500 each. Sell a high-end in-person mastermind to twelve people twice a year for $4167 each.

WAY 14

Assessments

People like assessments. They want to know more about themselves and others. I have good news for you! There are so many assessments already in existence; you don't have to create one from scratch. But if you want to create your own, it's not as difficult as you may think.

I remember how intimidated I felt when I decided to create my first assessment. Not so much by the questions and responses, but by the scoring and computing of results. So to make things easier, I used the bones of an assessment I liked and replaced the questions, choices, and results with my own information.

You can offer an assessment for a fee, like the DISC™ or Myers Briggs™ personality assessments, and that alone will put money in the bank. You can also offer the assessment for free and charge for the detailed results. Lastly, you can allow the assessment to be taken for free and give the results for free, but offer the prospect a fee-based coaching program to further explore their results (see Ways 5 and 19). When done well, any of those three options will make money.

There are all kinds of assessments, including:

✓ Marketing

✓ Communication

✓ Personality

✓ Business Acumen

✓ Social Skills

✓ Dating & Marriage

✓ Vocabulary

✓ Health

✓ Parenting Skills

✓ And more

The list is endless. You can create an assessment on just about anything you can think of. The key is delivering an assessment that your audience wants to take.

What would your ideal clients want to know about themselves?

I also encourage you to automate your assessments as much as possible. This will save you time, energy, effort, and money. Imagine someone coming to your website at 2:00 AM and taking your assessment. They enter their responses and the results appear on the screen or in their email. I recommend you require their first name and email address to receive their results so you can stay in touch with them and continue to build the relationship.

Another cool idea is to offer a free fifteen minute session to go over the assessment results. This works especially well if you are good at converting prospects to paying clients over the telephone. If you are not, it is a skill very worth practicing and perfecting.

How to Make $100K in One Year Example:

Charge $20 for your assessment and full results and get 5,000 people to sign up and pay. Offer your assessment for free in return for prospects' names and emails, then sell the detailed full results for $40 to 2500 of them.

15

Private Retreats

The interesting thing about offering a Private Retreat is not only that you can make money and provide learning *but* your attendees will love the break away from the rat race of their daily routine. Everyone is busy, tired, run down, stressed out, and here you come... to the rescue!

You can plan a getaway for some rest and relaxation or do a thematic retreat. The options are endless and should be based on your target market's interests and needs. The retreat can be structured where you have planned every minute of their time or semi-structured where they have planned activities and free time. Personally, I prefer semi-structured and my clients seem to like that balance as well.

How long should the retreat be? A two- to three-day retreat is popular, but a one-day retreat also works well when you market locally.

What unique activity or experience can you incorporate into the retreat?

The goal of a retreat is to deliver an *experience*. An experience your clients would be happy to pay for. When you step back and look at your client group, you may notice some similarities. If you take time to learn everything you can about your target market, you will know what they like. For example, *my* dream retreat would include some learning sessions, time being pampered at the spa, great food, and entertainment at a luxurious hotel that provides transportation from the airport (better yet, pick me up in a limo).

What comes to mind for you? Write that down—it's a good step in the direction of planning your retreat.

How to Make $100K in One Year Example:

Host two three-day retreats each year for a group of ten people and sell them for $5,000 per person. Host four small one-day local retreats to a group of twenty people and sell them for $1,250 per person. Increase the number of retreats you host to the same amount of people and you can lower the price.

WAY 16

Conferences

You've gone to a conference or two in your life and paid to be there, so why can't you put on a conference for your target market? No one says it has to be a huge multi-day event with numerous breakout sessions. A conference can be one single day where you are the only teacher.

People love live events. They want the opportunity to meet and learn from you in person as well as network with like-minded people in their industry. But when you think of a conference, don't envision the same old boring event where someone stands on stage and talks *at* the attendees all day long. Instead, make it a priority to create an experience for your attendees. You want them to talk about your event to everyone they encounter before, during, and after they attend.

Most people will not fill the room the first time you put on a conference, so I caution you to be careful when choosing a venue for your live event. You want a location that is convenient for attendees traveling by air. You want the venue to be as nice as you can afford without losing your shirt if attendance is not what you expect.

One of the first things I work on with my coaching clients is the creation or designation of their "signature program." This is the program or service you offer that sets you apart from everyone else in your industry and builds your strong brand. Unless you are so new to business that you don't have clients or customers, I am sure you already have something that can be turned into your signature program. Maybe it's a process you have developed over time to help your clients succeed. Hover over your business and look for steps or actions you take yourself or systems you have your clients use that helps them get from where they are to where they want to be.

Once you have identified your signature program, you have a foundation for what to teach at your conference. You can teach a little bit about each step in your signature program or you can choose the area you see most clients struggle with and teach an enormous amount on that topic. In other words, you need to go wide or deep. There is no right or wrong answer, so I recommend you begin with the end in mind:

✓ What do you want to happen after the event is over?

✓ What action do you want the attendees to take as a result of having completed your conference?

✓ What are you selling to your attendees?

Knowing what you want the attendees to do next will tell you whether to go deep or wide.

For example, my first signature program is called *Passion Won't Pay The Bills*. When planning my first live event, I knew my attendees would be fairly new to the Six Pillar concept I teach, so I decided to go wide. I did a one-day event where I spent about one hour on each Pillar. I wanted the attendees to enroll in my *Passion Won't Pay The Bills* program, which I offered in three versions: a six-week self-study, a six-month group coaching, or a private coaching opportunity.

Now it's your turn! What kind of live conference event can you do?

How to Make $100K in One Year Example:

Sell tickets to your conference to one hundred people for $1,000. Host two live conferences each year to one hundred people and drop that price to $500. Increase your attendees to two hundred people twice a year and sell tickets for $250.

WAY 17

Tutorials

Tutorials have been around for decades, but the Internet really opened the door to allow tutorials to be one of the fastest growing opportunities for adding money to your bank account.

People learn in different ways. Some like to watch, some like to listen, and some like to do, while others enjoy a combination. Add in the reality of people's busy schedules and you have a recipe for success. Notwithstanding the fact that tutorials allow you to "set it and forget it"—meaning create once and sell over and over again without having to do more work.

The purpose of a tutorial is to give your customer step-by-step instructions on "how to" do something. That something can be cooking, braiding hair, potty training, putting out a fire, laying carpet, changing a tire, bathing a baby, painting a house, etc. I guarantee you have knowledge that other people want to know, so teach it.

Tutorials come in all shapes and sizes to fit any topic you can imagine. They can be written with both words and pictures like a cookbook. Or they can be audio. I can't count the number of hours I have spent driving and listening to teaching CDs. When using this format, consider offering both the MP3 download and a physical CD option.

Tutorials can be virtual. I have a course for entrepreneurs called *Journey to Success*, where the participants receive one lesson each week via email with step-by-step written instructions on how to complete the recommended task.

These are all great opportunities for you and your prospective clients, but I want to share my favorite: video. Making videos is no longer expensive or complicated, plus they work *really* well for tutorials. And the greatest part of all is the technology now allows you to capture and record your computer screen. It also records audio so you can talk to your students while you perform the task.

There is nothing better than being able to hear and watch you perform each and every step.

Video tutorials differ from the standard teaching video where you are on screen talking to the viewer. Instead, imagine your clients sitting at their computer viewing your over-the-shoulder step-by-step video and performing the steps with you as they watch. They can pause and rewind your video as needed. My clients love when I offer video tutorials and I bet yours will too.

How to Make $100K in One Year Example:

Create and sell a written tutorial to 14,286 people for $7. Create and sell an audio tutorial to 5,008 people for $19.97. Create and sell a video tutorial to 2,128 people for $47.

Software

Have you ever wished there was an easier way?

How many times have you searched the Internet hoping to find a tool that would save you time, effort, energy, or money?

I know I have. I am guilty of spending hours looking for a resource that would automate a rote or technical task so I could stop being tortured by the duty. I have even asked around on forums and social media when I am desperate for a tool. Sometimes I am lucky and find exactly what I need. Other times I am quite disappointed. I'm sure you and your clients have the same experience.

Don't panic. I realize you may not have the skills to create software, but you can outsource the task to someone who does… once you know what you want.

What can you think of that would make your client's lives easier? Perhaps it's software that can effectively maintain client information. Sure, there are plenty of database products already on the market, but they may be missing a component that would be immensely helpful in your industry. Consider a tool you currently use. Is there a way to improve it or make it more user-friendly? If you have never considered software creation before, now is a good time to pay closer attention to your thoughts as you go about your daily work. You will undoubtedly come up with a few ideas that can help your clients.

Another software option which has become extremely popular is a mobile application. In this day and age nearly everyone has a smart phone. This provides a great opportunity for you to add another stream of income to your business.

How great would it be if your clients could access your information directly from their smart phone?

Here are some ideas of what you can deliver via your mobile application:

✓ A newsletter

- ✓ A magazine

- ✓ An e-book

- ✓ Audio

- ✓ Video

- ✓ Motivational quotes

- ✓ Tips

- ✓ A word of the day

- ✓ A series of lessons

The options are limitless, but keep in mind that the more complicated the mobile application, the more expensive it will be to create. So start with something simple unless you are growing money on a tree in your backyard.

Once you have your very own mobile application, you can give it away or charge a fee. In making that decision, start with the end in mind. What is your reason for creating a mobile application? What is your desired result?

One option is to make your mobile application free and deliver free content. This will grow your database of prospects, allowing you to offer items for sale as you build the relationship. The downside to this option is the increased number of "tire kickers" or "Lookie Loos" you will attract—people who just want free stuff.

A second option is to offer your mobile application for a nominal fee ($1–$10). You would still deliver high quality content, but you have also qualified your prospect by getting them to pull out their credit card and make a purchase. Even a $1 sale lets you know the person is serious about getting the knowledge you offer and will be much more likely to buy from you again.

A third option is to charge a higher price for your mobile application. This works well if you offer something of great value to your prospects and even better when marketed to people who already "know, like, and trust" you.

Creating a mobile application is not something you should rush into, but when you are ready it is an awesome idea.

How to Make $100K in One Year Example:

Create a mobile app to fill a major need in the marketplace and sell 50,000 downloads for $2 each. Create a free mobile app and advertise your other products or services.

19

Coaching or Consulting

You consider yourself a business owner, but why can't you add coaching and/or consulting to your offerings? Actually, you are likely already doing both, so you might as well make money at it.

There are many differing opinions on what a coach does vs. what a consultant does. And although I agree they have differences, they have valuable similarities, too.

Here's my opinion:

Coaching focuses on "the person." Consulting focuses on "the work."

Coaching helps the person with the "what." Consulting is about "how" the "what" will get done.

Coaching helps people find "direction." Consulting focuses on implementing "solutions."

Professionally, I prefer the word "coachsultant" because I truly believe the best service you can give your clients requires some of both.

Your client may benefit from coaching and once they discover their road to success, they have the ability to get there. Or your client may know exactly where they are going and benefit from consulting on how to get there with less time, money, energy, or effort. Or your client may benefit from a combination of the two.

So I challenge you to commit to serving your client in whatever way they need at the given moment. That means you meet them where they are and help them get where they want to go. Call it what you want, but do what it takes for your client to succeed.

Just like you, your potential clients may have a preconceived notion about what a coach does vs.

what a consultant does, and if you use the wrong word to describe what you do, you could be letting money walk out the door even though you are the best person to help them.

Let me ask you. How can you coach someone and then leave them on their own to figure out how to do what you told them they needed to do? Likewise, how can you tell someone how to do something they aren't sure they want to do? Does that help you understand why you need to offer both? In my business, I flow in and out of coaching and consulting and you can, too.

Some people see coaching as the talking and thinking work while consulting is actually doing the work. Under this definition, as a coach all you do is talk, but as a consultant you do the work for your client.

The varying definitions have a lot to do with the industry you serve. Taking time to understand your market's view of each word will help you offer the services they need in the right way, at the right time in the relationship. As long as you aren't married to one or the other title, you will succeed at being of service.

After all, isn't that the mission of your business?

How to Make $100K in One Year Example:

Create a coaching package of three thirty-minute sessions for $297 and sell 337 of them. Create a higher-end consulting package where you and your team do most of the work for the client and sell ten of them for $10,000.

20

Certification

Credentials are always a good thing to have and people want them, so why not create a certification program for your clients? The certification program will develop needed skills and increase your client's expert status, as well as yours. This is what colleges are made of, but certification programs are not only for the big boys.

The opportunities to certify are infinite. You have but to read the website of your local community college to find certificate programs in areas like plumbing, typing, childcare, dental hygienist, legal assistant, automotive, food service, medical assistant, youth development, etc. And guess what? A certification program can be delivered face-to-face or virtually via online instruction, audio or video, correspondence courses, classroom instruction, group study, webinars, workshops, or a hybrid of more than one.

A certification program is as simple as creating a curriculum that teaches students how to do something and testing to ensure they are capable of doing it well. There is a difference between a certificate of completion and certification. Unlike certification, curriculum-based certificates *usually* do not have ongoing requirements, do not result in an initial designation, and cannot be revoked. So before you jump into creating your certification curriculum, you must determine the goals of the program since they will guide the decisions you make.

If you are going to put your reputation on the line by certifying someone, you definitely want to make sure they have and *maintain* the skills and abilities you proclaim. Here are a few tips to guide you:

- ✓ Screen applicants to make sure they have the basic knowledge to be successful in the certification program.

- ✓ Administer a pre-test to determine what the learner already knows. Administer a post-test to determine what has been learned. *Data is golden.*

✓ Certification is not a group of random workshops; it is a series of comprehensive, logically sequenced, related topics that build a strong structure of knowledge and skills.

You should set a fee for certification as well as re-certification. Some certification programs also have an application fee, materials fee, and exam fees. One of the most interesting certification models also includes a monthly fee to maintain knowledge. This is a great way to add income to your certification program. The monthly fee could be for ongoing learning opportunities. For example, your certification program may require the learner to get sixteen hours a year of additional training to maintain their certification. The monthly fee could cover their registration in workshops you offer throughout the year. And yes, the ongoing training can be face-to-face or virtual.

Now... what can you add to the certification arena?

How to Make $100K in One Year Example:

Create a certification program for $3,000 with an added monthly continuing education fee of $47 and sell it to twenty-eight people. Create and sell a certification program for $2,000 to fifty people.

WAY 21

Licensing Rights

Licensing rights is a money making opportunity that not many business owners consider. Imagine having hundreds or thousands of people all around the world teaching your "signature program." It's like cloning yourself and spreading your message and your products like wildfire.

Think train-the-trainer. I imagine at some point in your career you have attended a train-the-trainer session. The author taught you how to teach their method, model, or process to others exactly like they would. Once you completed the train-the-trainer program, you received permission to teach their course along with the materials you need to be successful. You were also made aware of the legalities—the dos and don'ts of teaching the course and representing the author.

Think about entertainment, sports, and fashion— all areas where licensing rights are prevalent. You can offer licensing rights to a single workshop, conference, curriculum, your logo, etc.

As you build your business you will encounter clients who need a program or process because they don't have one or clients who love your curriculum so much they want to teach it. This is where licensing rights come in to play. You will also find the curriculum you initially developed for your market is transferable to other industries. For example, my *Passion Won't Pay The Bills* program was designed for CEOs running youth-serving programs, but it wasn't long before I realized my *Six Pillar System* was universal and could be applied to other industries. I have since used my system to grow other businesses like a barber school and auto-repair. I've also had coaches and consultants from other industries ask if they could use my system with their clients. When these revelations begin to surface, you know it is time to look at offering licensing rights.

Creating a licensing program is similar in nature to designing a certification program, but with the added legal permission that the licensee can use your property. Licensing rights also bear a larger price tag than certification because of its ability to produce money for the licensee. Licensing rights often include your books, assessments, forms, audios, videos, and any other tools the licensee will need to teach your program. As such, you can charge for the license as well as an ongoing monthly fee for access and use of your tools. And don't forget the annual renewal fee if they want to continue using your property. You will also get income from any of your products the licensee sells when teaching your program.

I must caution you, licensing rights is a legal process and I highly recommend you seek the guidance of an attorney. The last thing you want is to give permission for the use of your programs without a way to monitor and maintain the integrity of your name. Quality control is critical, but only you can decide what that looks like.

Here are a few things to begin your thinking process:

✓ Does the licensee need to have a certain amount of experience? If so, what kind?

✓ How long is the license good and is it renewable?

✓ Are they required to participate in additional learning?

✓ Do they have to purchase and complete your program as a student before they can apply for licensee status?

✓ Does the licensee need to be an entrepreneur? Do they need to serve a certain market?

✓ Will the licensee be required to teach your program face-to-face? Or can they also teach it virtually?

There is no right or wrong answer. This is your property and your licensing agreement, but don't get carried away with too many petty rules or you may not have any takers.

How to Make $100K in One Year Example:

License your program to twenty people each year for a startup fee of $4260, monthly fee of $20, and annual renewal fee of $500 per year.

Conclusion

Congratulations!

You now have 21 Ways to make $100,000 in one year, but don't get overwhelmed trying to tackle them all at once. Begin by adding to a product, program, or service you already provide. For example, if you currently offer teleseminars, create a package by repurposing the audio recording and including the transcript. Once you have maximized your existing products and services, you can branch out and include a few new Ways. For example, you can take the same teleseminar topic and begin speaking at conferences.

Keep in mind, the "How to Make $100K in One Year Examples" are just that—examples. The amount you charge for your products, programs, and services must be based on your market, your offer, and your level of expertise.

If you can bring $100,000 into your business with any one of the 21 Ways, imagine how easy it will be to bring $100,000 into your business if you use a combination of Ways.

Adding $100K to your income is simply a formula, but it begins by answering these questions. *And I want you to write your answers on paper.*

1. **"I need to survive!"** This is the bare minimum to pay your monthly bills and not have to get a J-O-B. This is not the income you want, but with some cuts in your lifestyle, the income amount you need to survive.

What is your monthly "I can survive" income number? $4K? $7K? $10K? More? **Your number $_____**

2. **"I can work with that!"** This is where you are not stressed or losing sleep. You are making enough money to easily cover your expenses without making sacrifices, and you no longer worry about getting a J-O-B. You are surviving just fine, but there is not enough for savings or *fun.*

What is your monthly "I am doing O.K." income number? $4K? $7K? $10K? More? **Your number $_____**

3. **"That would be nice!"** This is the monthly income that allows you to relax. You have more than enough to meet your expenses, contribute

to savings, and have some *fun*. At this level, you could be satisfied if you didn't make any more than this per month.

What is your monthly "I can relax" income number? $7K? $15K? $30k? More? **Your number $_____**

4. **"Ahh, my dream come true!"** This number says "I have arrived." You are wealthy and prosperous. You have achieved all your financial goals and can live the lifestyle of your dreams.

What is your monthly "dream" income number? $10K? $25k? $50k? $100k? More? **Your number $_____**

If you do the work and run the numbers, you can expect Big Business Results.

You can do this. Now it's time to take action!

$

About the Author

On stage, online and in her community, you can find Dr. Linette Montae - internationally acclaimed speaker, author and award winning results strategist - helping speakers, coaches and authors "leverage your platform, master your process and ignite your profit" but it wasn't so long ago that Dr. Montae *was a struggling CEO trying to make ends meet.*

You see, Dr. Montae had a good job with a great income and life was good. Until one day in September 2008, she was injured in a car accident after being t-boned on the driver's side of her SUV. During the 2 years that followed, she watched her cushy life blow up. In one year, Dr. Montae blew through all of her savings, her 401K, both of her IRA accounts AND every single penny of her emergency fund. She had 2 kids, with one leaving for college, and to add insult to injury, the bottom had fallen out of the economy and she could not find another job.

So she decided to start her own business. Easy, right?! Well, it was not as easy as she thought.

Dr. Montae has owned several businesses over the years but a lot had changed during her 5 years as an employee. When she jumped into being a business owner in 2010, she had no website, no email, no social media accounts, no autoresponder, and NO CLUE! During 18 months of being stuck in start-up with a bank account in the negative and working 80 hours a week IN her business, Dr. Montae experienced some hard but powerful lessons.

Here's some of what she learned:

- ✓ Passion Won't Pay The Bills
- ✓ Success Is A Decision (but you still have to do the work)
- ✓ Big Business Results Requires "Holistic-Strategic" Action
- ✓ STOP looking at the size of your business and START questioning the size of your results
- ✓ The Only Glass Ceiling Is The One YOU See!
- ✓ Strategies Without Systems Is Senseless

Now she uses her natural gift for being able to quickly zoom in on what's not working in your business, her professional experience coaching countless business owners from startup to success, and her doctoral education in Training & Performance Improvement helping entrepreneurs implement systems to increase profit so your business is THRIVING *and* you have more time to enjoy life!

Are you finally ready to STOP trying a bunch of stuff that costs too much, takes too long and doesn't work to grow your business?

In This Free Video I Am Going To Help You Build Your Unique "Take Passion Build Profit" Blueprint!

I can't wait to share . . .

- ✓ **What you need to build a business that gets BIG results!** *This is the same blueprint I use to customize my private clients road to success.*
- ✓ **The absolute WORST substance to use as the foundation for your business success!** *I see this mistake all the time.*
- ✓ **The 3 money makers that should be in every entrepreneur's business plan!** *Strategic Focus is key.*
- ✓ **The 2 most important things you MUST know and the #1 thing you MUST do for business success!** *Without all three, you are facing dismal results.*
- ✓ **The #1 task that can make or break your business**, *yet it is often the most overlooked!*
- ✓ **Exactly what to do when you have problems growing your business.** *It's probably not what you think but it works.*

If you keep doing the same thing, you can expect the same result!

Are You Ready For A Proven Plan to Build The Business of Your Dreams?

Visit
LinetteRecommends.com/TakePassionBuildProfit
and get your **free video** today!

Collect them all!

21 WAYS to **write & publish** your non-fiction **book**
Kristen Eckstein

21 WAYS to **powerfully network** your business
Kristen Eckstein

21 WAYS to enjoy a **stress-free holiday** season
Dr. Daisy Sutherland

21 WAYS to make **money speaking**
Felicia J. Slattery M.A., M.Ad.Ed.

21 WAYS to **skyrocket** your **creativity**
Tony Leidig

21 WAYS to be a **kid** again **& get adult results**
Kristen Eckstein

21 WAYS to **run** a **stress-free business**
Dr. Daisy Sutherland

21 WAYS to **manage** the **stuff** that **sucks up your time**
Grace Marshall

Look for more *21 Ways*™ books at
21WaysBooks.com

www.ingramcontent.com/pod-product-compliance
Lightning Source LLC
Chambersburg PA
CBHW071718210326
41597CB00017B/2525